PULLING WORDS
Nicholas Trandahl

Seth,

Best Wishes!

Winter Goose
PUBLISHING
where words take flight

Winter Goose Publishing
45 Lafayette Road #114
North Hampton, NH 03862

www.wintergoosepublishing.com
Contact Information: info@wintergoosepublishing.com

Pulling Words

COPYRIGHT © 2017 by Nicholas Trandahl

First Edition, April 2017

Cover Design by Winter Goose Publishing
Typesetting by Odyssey Publishing

ISBN: 978-1-941058-66-4

Published in the United States of America

To Brittany, Lily, and Holly

Contents

Heaven Happened Here   1
Quilt On The Driveway   2
The House Up On Pine Street   3
Evening Calling   6
Lilac Honey   7
Maybe Poets Are Not Liars   9
Cure From Kentucky   10
Decaying Qualities   11
Hyattsville   13
Seersucker   14
One Of A Great Many   16
Tangibility   18
Grand Themes   19
The Atlas I Stashed Away   20
Hours Of Light   21
A Poem About Majesty   22
Remember   23
Kicking Stars   24
Monday Evening   25
Sunday Morning Rhymes   26
Spirits   27
Fallen Apples (Importance)   29
She's Flickering   30
Heralding October   31
An Evening In Georgia   32
Spearfish Canyon   33
Historic Particles   34
Boston By Dawn   36

Crucible Of Patience   37
Driving After The Storm   39
The Sound Of Fall   41
The Sacrifice At Gay Head   42
Our Cairn   43
Just For You And I   44
Oak Bluffs   45
Bed And Breakfast   46
Nantucket Sound   47
Devout   48
Expectation In Revolt   49
Pieces Of Our Souls   50
How Can It Be So Hot?   52
Blue Ridge   53
The Days Of Autumn   54
Speaking With Stars   55
Patriarch   56
Hymn Of Hornets   58
Try To Remember   60
Fulfillment   61
Wanting   62
The Shades Of The Leaves   64
A Painting With No Name   66
Emptying The Well   67
Moons Like Embers   69
A Prologue To Winter   70
The Forgotten Taste Of Mulberries   71
You Don't Have To Worry About Breathing   72
Giving Thanks   73
A Devolution   74
Boy Soldiers   75

Recede 77

A Frosty Morning 78

Invincible 79

A Day Both Clear And Cold 81

Villainy 82

Midwinter 83

With What Was Thought To Be Benevolence 84

An Oblation 86

The Lengths We All Go 87

Invisible Wounds 88

A Grievance 91

Poetic Envy 92

In Hindsight 93

Things To Appreciate 94

Subtle Strokes 95

Chronologic Death Rattle 96

The Russians 97

Summer In Pokrovskoe 98

The Giver Of Gifts 99

A Poem For Carver 100

Stoicism And Assurance 101

Quietly Now 102

One's First Climbing Tree 104

Those Wild Ones 105

Replenishment 106

The Box Made Of Bone 107

What I Want 108

Just As Well 110

Architecture 111

Rain And Light 112

Until This Morning 113

Andromeda   114
Things Reminding Me Of Other Things   116
Thunder Basin   118
Belgium   119
The Only Voice I Hear   121
Horse Thief Lake   123
Prehistoric   126

Acknowledgments   127
About The Author   129

HEAVEN HAPPENED HERE

There's a warm campfire
flickering in the dark air—
staining the fresh scent
of newly-grown woods
with a serpentine banner
of drifting smoke.

I'm sitting around the fire
with the ones that I love,
passing around a flask
of sweet maple whiskey.
Our faces are crimson—
blemished by the firelight
and the spreading warmth
of the shared spirits.

Heaven happened here—

Didn't it?

That's why we're smiling,
why we laugh and love.

QUILT ON THE DRIVEWAY

It was nearly midnight
on a summer evening.
The memory tastes
as though it were August.

We spread out a quilt
on the driveway.

We weren't married yet—
only living together.
We were on our backs,
side by side,
patiently watching
the first celestial stirrings
of a meteor shower—
scattered diamonds
across the gulf of stars.
We kissed many times
because of the magic
inherent in the night.

I wonder if the stars
were keeping a tally
of our lips meeting,
of our wonderment
each time a silver streak
cut across the void,
of how many times
our two cats attacked us.

THE HOUSE UP ON PINE STREET

It was a small house, but adequate,
and it was nestled
on the wooded top of Pine Street.
It feels like I only lived there
for a part of a school year
and only a single perfect summer.
The divorce was as fresh as possible,
and I felt like an only child.
I just wanted to write stories and poems,
and I discovered the perfect writing spot
within a large shrub
of our overgrown backyard.
There was a small tunnel entrance
into that uncomfortable and blissful interior—
windows of perfect leaves
and sunshine stained yellow-green.

I would sit in that sylvan chamber,
writing in a brand new journal—
the cover of which was sheathed in green felt.
New journals were a precious commodity
in those hungry young days,
when winter was full and snowy
and the summer was verdant—
temperate.
These were days before the Oil Creek Fire
and before our normalcy was a dry prairie-
brittle and brown as shattered beer bottles.

This was before a blossomed devotion
to the wet delicious kisses of girls,
a time when my thoughts were pure
with creativity that was explosive and vibrant
and with innocent adventures with my friends.
We'd be riding our battered bikes
throughout the diminutive railroad town
that we had all memorized,
scratching words and symbols
in the concrete beneath the overpass
as coal-laden trains roared by us,
and buying comic books and pop
at the corner drug store—
that building is a bar now,
one of many that balance out
the number of churches in town.

I remember more of that summer
than I do scenes of my first marriage.
I can taste those summery old memories
in the whisper of a cool breeze
that washes into the afternoon stillness
of the modest home
within which I'm raising my own children.
It's a home down that very same idyllic street
that is edged in tall pines and cottonwoods—
many of which were broken and disfigured
by an early winter storm a few years ago.
In the crispness of the autumn
those cottonwood leaves turn as yellow as lemons,
and in the early days of summer

those boughs shed such a white deluge
of drifting tufts of cotton
that when I look straight up
into the sky of the clearest blue,
it looks like snowfall.

EVENING CALLING

A table is on the back deck,
covered in spread newspapers.
A bushel of blue crab is piled,
reddened shells and claws
caked in fragrant seasoning.
The brine of the Chesapeake
drifts into the citrus-hued air
of the golden summer dusk.

All of the frogs are croaking
down in the viridescent gloom
at the far end of the paddock.
Fireflies are rising and falling;
they're winking and glowing—
yellow-green, evening calling.

LILAC HONEY

Is there anything left on Earth
that is even worth waiting for?
I'll, right now, tell you there is.
You have only to be patient
through the cold winter months,
and through the blooming thaw
of March and April and May,
on up until we can discern
the sterling shores of June.

There is a fresh scent there—
in summer's sultry pregnancy.
You'll know it from your past,
those sepia-toned childhood days;
school had just ended for summer
and the warm days held nothing
but long hours of mirthful promise.
I also remember that fragrant aroma
from those same days of my own—
days of innocence and liberation.

Follow the toilsome honey bees
to those slender limbs that are heavy
with plush emerald leaves that harbor
pastel blossoms tightly bundled
at the ends of the bush's digits.
It's as though spring, in its last hour,
has offered us candy of soft amethyst,
candy sweetened without our ingenuity.

My children help me gather the blossoms,
fleeting though they are in June's birth,
and we gently rinse them in cool water,
before pressing them gently in dry linen—
that fabric's another summer scent,
sheets billowing in a balmy breeze.

Overnight, the purple blossoms impart
their notes that are citrusy and floral
into amber-hued honey that fills a jar.
In the morning, we spread the honey
over the crisped surface of toast,
like spreading gold and gems on a table.

The trick is to get a sticky blossom
in each and every delicate bite.
On the toast, the blossoms will be brown
after spending the night in honey.
Those fine petals will be stained
like the antiqued hue of a memory.

MAYBE POETS ARE NOT LIARS

There are real things
and there are unreal things.
A spider is there,
traversing my knee
like a mountain summit,
and there are wishes
flying around like little birds
with no nest to land upon.
I think of both things,
real and unreal,
and I write about both things
as if I know them.

But maybe poets are not liars.

Maybe we only want
to show you everything
all around you,
even the things that we,
ourselves,
have never even seen.

CURE FROM KENTUCKY

My lips kiss the rim
of a tumbler,
cool with ice.

A cherrywood-hued
finger of bourbon
is thrown back
into my throat.

It slides down
like a hot coal,
breaking through
different things
on the way down.

DECAYING QUALITIES

Seated in the sunlight again,
early afternoon—
a cold wind is whispering
that I've got nothing to do yet,
no task in need of completion.
I'm reading Mary Oliver
because there is no poet on earth
better to read
in the quiet sunshine.
I'm reading about how
a deer nudged her hand
as she sat in a summer meadow.
I, on the other hand,
have to lure deer to my lawn
by leaving slices of apple
hidden away in the grass.
I've so much to learn
about stillness—
about peace and devotion.
My house sits in the heart
of a tiny town—
old Merino,
older Irontown.
It sits like a grouse nest
in the sage and shale,
just to the southwest
of the Black Hills
that are, in truth, green.

I'm taking this place for granted.
But when, as a child,
we would visit
and eventually relocate,
there was a piney scent
and also an aroma of dry stone.
This town once had a demeanor
of peace and allegiance
that I can no longer sense.
Did these qualities decay,
or, these many years later,
have I decayed?
The church that rests
across the silent intersection
has a swirling dust devil
in its empty parking lot,
and I see the childish irony
in that observation.
Smirking, I take another drag
from my sweet cigar.
The sidewalks are crumbling,
but that's just fine.
That's what stone does
against the superiority
of invincible time.
Everything is much more solid
when bolstered
by the strength of the past—
when tucked safely away
in the forgotten corners
of our memories.

HYATTSVILLE

Latin American workers
ignoring me as I pass,
in my quest
for garter snakes.
There were always
serpents to find
under plastic pots.
Strolling the floral rows
of a botanical nursery
as a young child,
I was struck by
the pungent aroma
of marigolds
and zinnias—
the Maryland sunrise.

And I carry it with me still,
as a man—
wherever I go.

SEERSUCKER

In vertical pastel hues,
striped with white,
each button-front shirt
hangs in its state
of perpetual dishevelment.
My closet is lined with them,
like articles of pale candy,
like the promise of a trip
to a hot and humid clime
that errant time
has borne me to.

Is my fair frame thus clothed,
in these fantasies,
as I swagger in the Deep South—
where everything is white and green,
swampy,
slick with a slime
of charm, history, and guilt?
Could I see the Mississippi sunset
that Faulkner saw
as he traded barbs about lexicon
with Papa Hemingway?

Or am I in India,
the birthplace of said fabric
to combat the womb
of all the world's sweltering air?

Would I be chewing naan,
standing easily on an old balcony,
thinking of Buddha
and all the hungry ghosts
as I stare towards the tall north—
emerald foothills
with ghostly heights beyond them,
bluish-white in the dim distance?

Or do I wear them
back to my roots—
to Rappahannock
and the slumbering Blue Ridge,
where I can attempt to discern
who I am—
and why?
Should I be kneeling
before an old wooden fence
that's completely shrouded
in blossoming honeysuckle vine—
worshiping at the altar
of nostalgia
and trying to find the genesis
of how each of my words
came to pass?

These promises we make—
what weight they carry.
And how unassumingly they hang,
waiting for us to reach out
and finally don them.

ONE OF A GREAT MANY

The heat of the summer sea breeze
as it traveled over the flat farmland,
studded with rumbling old tractors.

That breeze rustling yellow flowers
as a train full of Londoners on holiday
raced in cheerfully from the east.

The murmur of sapphire-hued waves
that caress the feet of eroded cliffs
and lick the bustling sandy beaches.

A cozy seaside cottage stained by salt,
gilded in colorful fragrant flowers.
Eggs, milk, bread, and cheese
have been freshly bought,
and they're waiting for me,
resting in shade upon an antique table.

I was in Cornwall.

But only because the British romance novel
was so remarkably vivid.
It was as though, in opening the book,
my face was licked by summer wind.
I felt as though I'd finally returned
to somewhere strikingly familiar.

I've learned that Cornwall is a home,
one of a great many,
in which I have yet to set my stride—
but yearn to.

TANGIBILITY

The erection and collapse
of sun-licked ocean waves
has done more to illuminate
a ravenous and eager soul
than any construct of man—
any deity's honeyed words.

GRAND THEMES
For Craig Eutsler

I am very unsure
if grand themes
are as deserving
of honest prose
as simple things—

the quiet light
painting the edges
of melting ice
in my drink—

the seagrass
softly whispering
in Atlantic air—

the poetic collapse
of cottonwood leaves,
yellow like fire—

putting a finch,
tragically silenced,
into the earth—

two young boys
placing pennies
on train tracks
made warm
by the July sun.

THE ATLAS I STASHED AWAY

I still think we should go
on that road trip to Seattle.
Our route remains highlighted
in the atlas I stashed away.
I don't want to open it up
and find our sojourn faded
with time's irredeemable press.

It's been so many years,
but I can still imagine it;
we finally behold the skyline
through the pines and clouds.
We see the ships, white and red,
that are upon Puget Sound
like salt in cobalt tides.
Listening, we can faintly hear
their muffled bells and horns
through the soupy murk.

We can make more memories
to embroider on our souls.
We can have a new adventure.

I'm going to look for that atlas.

HOURS OF LIGHT

Indifference.

The evening holds, literally,
nothing for me.

Give me hours of light.

Give me that steady tide
by which I rise and read,
and by which I write
all the best words
that I can pull from the sky
and its kaleidoscope of colors.

A POEM ABOUT MAJESTY
Dedicated to Mary Oliver

Is there really more majesty
upon the frozen summit of a peak,
beneath the mighty press of the sea,
within the fury of molten stone,
before a frenzied rush of wind,
than in the lilting complexities
of a songbird's joyful melody?

I don't truly believe that there is,
but I haven't the majesty to decide.

REMEMBER

I remember a stone
that was smothered
in a mass of ladybugs.
Chilled overcast air,
clouds heavy
on green mountains.
Was it spring or fall—
a chilly summer day perhaps?
I can't even imagine
which American environ
my feet trod upon.

Is this a memory,
or is this a dream?
All that I know is . . .

I remember it.

KICKING STARS

Kicking sapphire stars on Rehoboth Beach—
moonlight glittering in a confetti of sand
tossed from nude toes, only five years old.
We walked together as a family, all of us,
like I remember us doing in the Appalachians,
before we happened upon that black snake
that was sunning on the winding dirt trail;
before the fighting, the screams in the car,
hair being pulled and promises of divorce;
hoping, more than anything, that it all—
wasn't over.

MONDAY EVENING

I watch her,
a woman I love,
teach my daughter
about vinyl records
and how the record player works.

I make a gin and tonic—
watching.
Smiling.

I can't keep my love quiet.

SUNDAY MORNING RHYMES

Countless shards of sugary morning light,
stained all in yellow and luminous white,

> press through windows, curtain and lace,
> dappled and hushed, lucent upon my face.

An incandescent elixir is Sunday's rich glow.
A bloom of its soft qualities begins to grow.

> My soul drinks of it, swallowing deeply,
> using it quietly, wielding it discreetly.

SPIRITS

The prairie is blistered
in the dry Wyoming air.
The smell of sage
and raw earth permeates.
My friend and I,
maybe two decades
shared between us,
go to help his dad
operate a cattle branding.
We went by a rattlesnake
on the way there.
That snake and I
were the least violent ones
on the prairie that day.
A congregation
of tall cowboys,
faces and hands
like brown leather,
searing captive fur and flesh
with scalding red-grey iron—
proclaiming
the property of life.
Panicked bovine moans
and eyes stretched wide
in confusion and pain.
A knife slick with calf blood—
testicles sizzling
on the cast-iron stove

that heats the branding irons.
Few of these stoic cowboys
are brave enough
to take a nibble.
Some, however,
are far too brave.
They've something to prove
to one another.

My friend and I,
both dirty and weary
with ranch work,
are given a small glass bottle
of blackberry brandy
to pass back and forth
in his dark, dusty basement.
We take nervous sips—
commemorating steps into manhood,
into work and control,
into violence,
and into sweet dark spirits
that take the burnt edge
off of life.

FALLEN APPLES (IMPORTANCE)
For Christopher O'Bryan-Pitcher

There are blossoms
as important to the bee
as to the florist;
lighthouses as important
to sensitive souls
ambling the unquiet shore
as to the wayward vessel
plowing through high seas;
fallen apples
as precious to artists
with transcendent ideals
as to the orchardist
or even the peckish doe—
a pair of skittish fawns
trailing behind her.
There are people
of more importance
to distant friends
than faces seen daily.

SHE'S FLICKERING

A Parisian morning,
an outdoor café—

Her breath marked
with *eau de vie.*

A journal opened,
pen at the ready.
She's awaiting prose
that flutters down
from the lemony sky
like dust in sunlight,
like butterflies,
or like moths—

She's flickering.

HERALDING OCTOBER

The leaves like bejeweled fire—
ruby, amber, opal, and topaz,
glittering in the copious boughs,
lavish with their warm jewels.

We welcome October
and a delicate firmament.

AN EVENING IN GEORGIA

A spring night in the Georgia woods,
an hour or two after a powerful rain.
But now the air is opened and clear,
a great sweep of bluish-white stars
strewn across the immense heavens
like the hot spent shells of a rifle.
I'm on guard duty, my platoon prone,
slumbering soundlessly in orderly rows.

In the humid distance there is a chorus,
snarls and barks of roving feral dogs.
Alone, that was awful enough to hear,
to witness the carnivorous echoes.
But then the shrill scream of a wild hog
blooms from the canine cacophony.
For too long the hog shrieks in horror.
When its pained cries are finally muted,
the pack too grows silent.
I imagine the beasts splitting flesh
and lapping up hot gore.

I think then that some of us soldiers
are like the dogs, the fast hunting pack
maneuvering in the Fort Benning night,
and some of us are the lone hog—

Doomed and victimized.

Consumed.

SPEARFISH CANYON

For Chase Ambler

The aspens are shining—
golden and gleaming
like precious ore,
all that lost yellow
concealed betwixt
the robust green of pine
and the towering walls of stone,
some of which
are weeping waterfalls—
brilliantly white.
The aspens rattle their white arms—
whispered music
lovingly painted
with the crisp words of autumn.
Each of those fiery manes
is, in fact, an appendage
of a single grand entity,
strewn together by roots.
What greater metaphor exists,
what larger example
of togetherness,
than the unifying lesson
taught by the aspens?

HISTORIC PARTICLES

There are antique buttons
in some small shelves I own.
I've collected all kinds,
old glass and Bakelite,
but there are some
as golden yellow as anything
luminescent and sweet.
I spill just those yellow ones
out on a smooth wooden surface—
organize them,
rearrange them for no reason.
In the warm morning sun
those buttons look like honey
spread out on a biscuit—
steam rising,
new laughter around a table.
They look like apple juice—
sugary droplets frozen by time.
The buttons look like
the summer sun of Italy
opening a buttery eye
over Venice—
glittering in the canals.
I hear the gondoliers sing.
I'm roaming the *sestieri*
and wishing for a quiet home
somewhere in *Cannaregio*,
enough away from the throngs

clogging the Grand Canal
to be happy.

Can you see now
why I collect these old buttons—
why I hoard historic particles?

BOSTON BY DAWN

We wait—

tiredly lingering
among the hordes
bound for Boston.

We wait—

to fly up into
the clear crisp
autumn night.

We wait—

to readily skewer
the fiery bloom
of the rising sun.

CRUCIBLE OF PATIENCE

Still waiting
for the fog to break.
The pilot, in shirtsleeves,
comes into the gate
looking like he himself
built the awaiting aircraft
and has been shaking his fist
at whatever entity
controls the fog.
Another fifteen minutes,
he tells the woman
behind the desk.
This is agony—
the wait,
the exhaustion.
Is this some sort
of purifying trial,
forcing us to prove
our devotion and loyalty
to this adventure?
This is, in fact,
a crucible of patience.

But we will succeed.
We will reach the island.

She sleeps.
I wait.

Silence.

My mind feels like
the fog outside
the airport windows.

DRIVING AFTER THE STORM

In the grim half-light
we leave in the car.
Driving down the road,
the forest is brightening—
trees shaken by the storm,
their fallen leaves hugging
the damp asphalt.
The overcast sky
is being torn asunder
by the flagrant heart
of this new day.
Moss shrouds the oaks.
The air smells like promise.
We can't stop smiling—
shadows dappling the car.
There is sand on the road—
oceanic deposits in the forest.
The smell of the air
after the morning's storm
blends seamlessly
with autumn's spicy scent
and the distant trace
of the salty Atlantic.

Deep woods,
roads winding through them
as if through mossy tunnels,
give way to bogs and dales,

old moss-covered stone walls,
and then, finally,
the darkened blue of the Atlantic
off the island's west shore.
The wind is blowing
in off the sea.
The briny fresh scent
stirs me with memories
of my childhood.
The salt in the air
scrubs from my life
all of its mundane trappings.

Nothing at all
will be mundane again.

THE SOUND OF FALL

Up island, October's deft wizardry
has rusted the brambles and shrubs
into a scarlet color as rich as blood.

If one stands still on the sandy trail,
closing their eyes and only listening,
the raspy grandfatherly sound of fall
may come whispering in from the east,
a voice upon the crisp autumn breeze
as it races across the whole of the isle
in a quest for attentive observers.

THE SACRIFICE AT GAY HEAD

The edifice is perched precariously,
its scarlet eye silently winking
atop the cliffs of flesh and bone—

up island.

Neptune awaits patiently below.
Looking up, he is famished, greedy.
He demands a suitable offering—

a sacrifice.

A seal, headless and sun-bleached,
rests in the sand far down below,
a feast for a single wary gull—

a glutton.

The tide will come pouring in,
finding the seal and not the cliffs.
Neptune collects the putrid flesh—

the offering.

The edifice yet remains.

OUR CAIRN

We stacked sandy stones,
and made a monument
in the kind shadow
of an old lighthouse,
a monument of love—
of our devotions.

We think of our tower
of sea-smoothed stones
that are even now
soaking in the glow
of the setting sun
that spills over Aquinnah.

Our cairn is evanescent,
but it will, for us,
stand for all time.

JUST FOR YOU AND I

The azure sky over Vineyard Haven brightens
through the uncovered skylight of the room.
How can this possibly be the same vast sky
that is stretched taut over all other lands?

How can this not be a special sky—
a sky just for you
and just for I?

Lover, let us awaken with the gulls.

OAK BLUFFS

These still-green oaken crowns
are swallowing all of autumn.
These perfect old trees blush
in tones of amber and scarlet,
and big grey squirrels chatter
and scamper down the trunks.
There's a small candy shop,
and a place to buy colored pencils.
There's a spot to eat croissants
on an absolutely perfect beach,
with ravenous gulls as pedestrians.
These narrow streets are quiet,
the quaint Victorian homes pastel.
This harbor, at dusk, is pastel too,
and strewn with slumbering boats.

This is where I left my heart,
so that one day I can return—

to find it.

BED AND BREAKFAST

A house spider
skirts the wall of the room.

It belongs here.

It is an islander.

Later, walking alone
down towards the harbor,
I pass tourists.
I look down at my oxfords
as I walk.
I gaze at houses
with feigned nonchalance.

In my sweater,
my hair tousled by wind
that streaks up the hill
from the azure sea,
I pretend that I too
am an islander—
like the spider at the inn.

I don't take photos.
I buy a bag of groceries,
and walk back
to the room.

NANTUCKET SOUND

We were safe there,
at the cobalt ocean—
jellyfish avoided like
pellucid landmines.

The seabirds ascended
into the cerulean ether.

We greedily necked
in the dry beach grass,
eager for the fallen dark
and our concupiscent acts.

DEVOUT

As we departed State Beach Park,
sand in our hair and love on our lips,
we saw a large pond in the rich glow
of the antiqued autumn afternoon.

There were large houses perched
on the far side of it like old castles,
guarding, with privilege, that bath
of shimmering sunshine and gold.

We were devout believers, you and I,
in the molten light of the plunging sun
that poured into Sengekontacket Pond
and smeared it with warmth and magic.

EXPECTATION IN REVOLT

Quaint expectations
were in revolt.

An ominous syringe
jutted precariously
from the sandy shore
like a horrid blemish—
the afternoon glow
shining through
its dirty glass
like crystal.

An offer for sex
was scrawled
on an empty white wall
of a public restroom
behind the book store—
close by the harbor.

What would that night bring?
Who would be waiting
on the bench outside
when ten o'clock
settled over the island?

PIECES OF OUR SOULS

We leave pieces of our souls
in each and every place we go,
and I want to leave so many pieces
in all the most beautiful places.
I've left sizeable slabs of myself
upon this island—
its breezy shores and full woods.
And I'll go home possessed of it,
its touch ever sewn into heart.

When I have returned home—
back to the faded sagebrush,
to the shale and colorless grass,
to the leafless cottonwoods,
to the oil wells and coal mines
that crack the sunset's palette
and I'm driving across the grassland
to some distant point,
to all those familiar faces—
I will softly prod the island
that's concealed within me
like a glowing aquamarine jewel.

At my desk I will smile, sighing,
and recall the salty sea air,
the taste of freshly-caught lobster,
our salacious nights at the inn,
the voice of the thundering waves

that ate away South Beach,
walking out on the jetty
upon the slippery stones—
barefoot, my khakis rolled up,
hunting for the brittle empty shells
that once belonged to horseshoe crabs,
the two of us, in sweaters,
strolling through quaint towns,
wandering to Edgartown Lighthouse
in the brisk light of a fiery sunset.

Leaving here is bittersweet.
I'm letting go of something
that's become quite important to me.
I am choking down sobs as I smile,
and, gazing at her,
I can see that she feels
the exact same way as I.

We've both left behind
pieces of our souls.

I am windblown.

I am forlorn.

I am jubilant.

HOW CAN IT BE SO HOT?

After the honeymoon,
I take a bottle of champagne
out of the fridge.
I amble outside
where my kids play
and my wife smokes
a flavored cigar.
I pop the cork
into brittle tan leaves
heaped in the dry lawn,
and I slurp down
the swiftly rising foam.
My lips and my beard
can't catch it all.
The children watch,
laughing,
and so do the wasps
that lazily bump
into our windows.
They've been made sluggish
by the lateness
of the year.
How can it be so hot
in late October?

BLUE RIDGE

An enormous copperhead
was brutalized by a canoe oar.
I would pluck honeysuckle
and catch fireflies,
their scent on my digits—
sometimes on the same day.
Did anyone wash their hands
in those days?
We'd walk our horse paddock,
finding Civil War bullets.
Tadpoles, frog eggs,
and unhealthy sunfish
populated our small pond.
And yet there I was,
a patient red and white bobber—
watchful.

The old Blue Ridge
were out of view
and yet . . . still there—
watchful.

THE DAYS OF AUTUMN

The days of autumn—
they fall like leaves
from boughs colored in warmth,
smoldering against the cooling air.

The days of autumn—
like those hot-toned leaves—

blaze with evanescence.

SPEAKING WITH STARS

The stars had always been
the most sentimental of friends.
Glittering like splintered gems
in the grand loft of the night,
they spoke very softly
of reassurance.

The stars sparkle even now,
years later, over a bleaker world.
But their voices have, for me,
become muted—
like the love of man
for one another.

Are they saddened, those stars,
or are they angry with all of us?
I wonder if the stars will dim
as they, one by one, turn away
from our little blue planet,
recasting their celestial gazes—
elsewhere.

PATRIARCH

I think of you alone in the Bighorns,
sipping schnapps from a metal flask,
hopefully a good book in your pack
with your extra ammunition and gear.
I think of your unspoken lessons,
quiet and visceral things
that your presence alone imparted.

I remember a knife, dark in the cool air,
cutting open the innards of a dead grouse—
bloodied fingers pushing out clumps of sage,
still dry and aromatic, recently swallowed.
Then the odor of a gutted and skinned deer
hanging in the rafters of the dusty garage,
clotted blood darkening old newspapers
spread out on the concrete floor.

I remember my spinner glinting in the sun,
shimmering at the end of my trained cast
into Sand Creek, hoping for a trout to strike.
Years earlier, from that same deep creek,
I caught a bottom-feeder, a slow bullhead.
I've scarcely been as proud as I was then.
You encouraged that pride, Father,
and you cooked that bony fish for me,
so that I could haughtily eat my catch.
Has anything ever tasted as good?

I remember living in cities and rural towns,
from Virginia to the plains of Wyoming,
seemingly without my tall rustic patriarch.
Even your family wasn't enough to keep you.
Distant woods, flaxen fields, and pure air
called to you, beckoned you away from us.
I think that all of the pheasants, ducks, and deer
cried to you in primal voices louder than ours.

Father!

Father!

Father!

I remember the few predawn awakenings,
nervous in the cab of one of your old trucks—
small fingers scratching anxiously at the seat.
We crept prone up a prairie embankment,
you guiding my aim before the trigger pull,
and a turkey slowly fell forward to death.
We were duck hunting in the morning,
crouching beside Labradors in reeds,
wearing autumnal camo and blaze orange.
You issued an order to fire as the ducks flew.
I knew you were jubilant as the gun broke the air
and a single mallard faded from the flock.

My father, be proud that, even in these changed days,
with written words and a pen in lieu of bullets and guns,
I still haven't missed a shot.

HYMN OF HORNETS

The Middle East—
the sky, at night,
was a starless haze.
One would wish it
filled with something
to adorn the foreign gloom.
I used to imagine the desert sky
as a menagerie of heavenly bodies,
but all we truly had
was the amber glow
of generator-run lighting
and the winking lights of cargo planes.
There were some nights, however,
while working a twenty-four hour shift
on the tactical site,
when I would find myself alone—
outside in the hot, humid night.
The roar would begin—
dimly—
far away.
But then it would escalate
to the volume of a continuous blast,
protracted to a length of ten minutes.
Standing there
in the cooling birth of the night,
listening to a squadron of F-18s
ascend up into the Persian firmament,
I was enchanted—

mesmerized,
and I was enchanted yet
when the slow, yellow-orange burn
of the rising sun
bloomed in the Asian east,
searing through the brown haze—
when the Hornet squadron returned
from Afghanistan skies—
deprived of their thunderous payloads.
I was thankful to those pilots
for ornamenting the night,
for heralding the dark
and the light.

TRY TO REMEMBER

I try to remember
every gilded leaf,
each oaken deposit
that October settled
upon that quiet lane.

I try to remember
those fallen leaves
like the final words
of a dying loved one,
each separate item
equally precious—

equally sacred.

FULFILLMENT

Something within me is thrilled
at unseen geese honking overhead,
heralding November in Wyoming
and the poignant passing of a year.

So suddenly the day is attained.

WANTING

Does solitude find us wanting,
reaching out in desperate fervor
for one to quench a social thirst?

I've buried my roots deep down.
They're tangled betwixt stones and sins
of the misty and melancholic past.

And I also reach joyfully skyward,
adorned digits raking at a future
that's rosy with a sublime glow.

Seeds fall from me;
sprouts burst forth.

I am not wanting;
solitude could not find me.

It will never find me until I go,
alone and weary of the Earth,
into death, and I embrace it
as the old estranged friend it is.

My roots, they also reach out
in the same manner as my fingers—

reaching out for something—

Anything.

Nothing.

My roots meet the roots of another,
and, like aspen trees, we're one—

bodies apart—

separated by the indomitable press
of a world that is cold and aloof.

And yet, I repeat,
we are one.

And solitude will never find me—

wanting.

THE SHADES OF THE LEAVES
An Autumnal Requiem

Fondly—
I remember yellow;
the birch leaves shivering in the crisp air,
thirsty cottonwoods shining like treasure—
       blazing like fire.

Contentedly—
I remember orange;
the stained oak leaves ablaze in October,
boldly-hued pumpkins in furrowed fields—
       later to be carved into faces.

Anxiously—
I remember scarlet;
the rusty boughs of sugary maples,
hot blood poured from a hunted stag—
       beneath a bloody sunset.

Bitterly—
I remember brown;
the venerable trees, angular and nude,
turkeys stalking warily in leaves—
       dead and brittle.

Sullenly—
I remember grey;
the clouds above, thick and blanketing,
dreary cold fog at dawn, seasoned—
       the smoke of smoldering leaves.

A PAINTING WITH NO NAME
For Wendy McWilliams Burdick

The first one melted,
cooked in the arid heat
of a Wyoming summer.

But then another came,
the second painting—
a painting with no name.

A blackened monolith—
an acidic sky above,
stained in yellow ochre.

I can turn it upside down
and behold the Jazz Age,
Fitzgerald's glittering mirage.

I wander here often,
seated at my desk,
because of her painting.

EMPTYING THE WELL

Somewhere there is a well.
Once, it was full of ink,
and every grim forlorn line
that he jotted in a journal
lowered the level a bit more.

That lost well, wherever it is,
is entirely dried up now,
but there are blackened wounds
revealed at the bottom of it.
They're wounds that won't heal,
and things like crass vermin,
stones plummeting bitterly,
and melancholic downpours
can irritate and open them
so that they shed more ink.

It's his sacred duty to write,
to quickly pen more lines—
to purge that dark seepage
so that the level of ink lowers.
But it's so much harder now
to find new ways to express
that too-familiar darkness.
What new words are there?
Are there any new ways
to write them down?

It's his duty to seek relics
that sensitivity can locate—
things like radiant sunshine,
things ethereal and sylvan,
things that make it easier
to ignore the well.

MOONS LIKE EMBERS

I spoke with one of my daughters
about how a moon can be orange
and even a burgeoning crimson.

Harvest Moons.

Blood Moons.

Moons that shine like fire.

Driving home through the unlit night,
a rich glow shone over the horizon
like the illumination of a nearby town.
But, rounding the silhouette of a hill,
I beheld a moon as brightly orange
as the hottest of flaring embers.

I wished that she was with me,
but I hoped, wherever she was,
that her gaze was skyward.

A PROLOGUE TO WINTER

Standing in detritus that is crystallized,
I gaze up into the leafless boughs.
The firmament is the grey of impure pearls,
and the darkened limbs are contrasted
against the lurid void like cracks—
like fractures across its delicate purity.
Each blackened trunk, then, is like a rift,
a chasm in the glassy expanse.

The year is falling into a cold death,
falling like the leaves that once adorned
still branches that are now quiet and bare—
immodest.

Sleep, autumnal days.

Sleep.

THE FORGOTTEN TASTE OF MULBERRIES

All five of our senses
don't attend each and every
poignant meeting of memory.

I can fondly remember,
as a youth in rural Virginia,
loving the flavor of mulberries,
just freshly-plucked
from a healthy branch,
heavy with fruit.

My mouth yet waters,
even though, sadly,
I can't recall the taste.

YOU DON'T HAVE TO WORRY ABOUT BREATHING

Dedicated to Ernest Hemingway

"'That's why I like it better underwater,' David said.
'You don't have to worry about breathing.'"
—Ernest Hemingway, *Islands in the Stream*

These waves
lack clemency.

They're engorged
with plight.

What peace
there must be—

deep down
in the sea's womb.

I smile in anticipation
of the descent.

GIVING THANKS

Like a king upon frozen battlements,
I stand on the front step, in tweed,
straightening my thin burgundy tie
and hurriedly smoking a small cigar.

The snowscape around me appears
as white flames beneath the noon sun,
but the breeze, seasoned with winter,
bites my dry hands with an icy kiss.

Bells at the Methodist Church ring out
into the cold fragility of the air.
Chimney smoke threads its way up
from where families begin to feast.

I am hungry and I am thankful.

A DEVOLUTION

You and I, we are now actors
at work upon a new stage.
Discrepancies are ignored,
as they always have been.
We pretend to forget them—
to diminish them.

Very quietly, just like that,
a devolution occurs between us.
Suddenly, we are acquaintances.
We burn bridges with aloof smiles,
abhorrently uncaring of what we do.
We wear the shards of our history—

Days of glory.

Days of youth.

BOY SOLDIERS

Think of us back then.
Two young boys, brothers,
pretending to be soldiers—
intoxicated by warfare.

How we wanted Bull Run
and the bloody horror of Antietam,
blue and grey woolen uniforms
stained with scarlet blooms.
How we wanted to pilot Phantoms
fast and low over the jungle,
dropping napalm as we went
and dodging anti-aircraft fire.
How we wanted to walk rice paddies
with M-16s cradled in our hands,
our eyes peeled for Vietcong.

Our patrols and maneuvers
would take us across our paddock,
into the woods behind the pond,
or through the rows of trees
comprising our shelterbelt.
Our packs would be too large
for our antique equipment
and the salted crackers
we pretended was hardtack.
We would be out the whole day—
wouldn't we?

Think of us back then,
kids trying their hand at war
in the quietness of rural America,
and then think of where we ended up—
you in a life-or-death struggle
at any bar that would let you in,
with legions of emptying bottles
and hardened knuckles—
split and bloodied;
me choking to the edge of death,
a government-issued belt
tightened around my throat,
in a darkened barracks rooms
somewhere in the Middle East.
We've always been soldiers,
hunting for that violent drama—
one way or another.

Think of us back then,
and see if you can discern
any clue of what was to come.

RECEDE

Recede, night. Recede.
Bathe me in light—

in radiance.

I want a fierce brilliancy
that sears deep to my bones,
bearing me like a torch—

an open flame.

I want pure illumination—

enlightenment.

I want the whole enormity
of the vast delicious world;
I want it to change me—

to purify me.

Recede, night. Recede.
For I desire a discourse
with that which supplants you—

with the usurper,

with the dawn.

A FROSTY MORNING

The sun-drenched dawn is aglitter
in a crisp shroud of gleaming rime.

Like ghosts, deer pass silently by,
muzzles disturbing the delicate frost
as they search for fallen apples.
It looks like they breathe smoke,
their exhalations painted by cold.

The junipers are quietly blemished
with a fragile dusting of pale frost,
a niveous salt nightly granted.
They shine with incandescence
and barely shed their teal aroma.

What an elegant and ethereal brush
nature deftly wields.

It's like the pen of a poet in love.

INVINCIBLE
A poem for my wife

I think of all the things
that started with you.
It's like I had never
written a word before
or read anything
truly beautiful.
But then, in October,
we were married—
orange, yellow,
scarlet, and brown—
faces of the leaves.

Later, on the beach,
I stood behind you.
You were in a long skirt
that clung to your curves,
and your feet were bare—
your sandals in my hands.
You had waded
through the shallow surf
and stood upon
a lonely rock.
Facing the setting sun
that turned Vineyard Sound
into a sea of shining opal,
you giggled out loud
like a child
first seeing the ocean.

Standing on the shore,
I watched you—
the most lovely thing
that I had ever seen.

You gave a simple comment
when we ate chowder
at a seaside tavern
in New England.
I feel invincible,
was what you uttered.
It may have been
an odd statement
to say between bites,
but I knew exactly
what you meant.

Before I gazed
into your large eyes,
it's as though
I had never seen
the rich hues
of dark chocolate.
Before your embrace,
I feel as though
I had never made love.
It used to be so difficult
to find the things
that needed written about,
but now . . .

poetry.

A DAY BOTH CLEAR AND COLD

My breath slipped
from my chapped lips
in frosty plumes.

It was a clear day—
a radiant day.
But the air
was sharp enough
to pain my nose and ears—
both reddening.

All around me
were gentle hills
glazed in snow—
pristine and gleaming
in the frigid glare
of the winter sun.

Was there a point
to all of this?
Did there need to be?

Sometimes it's better
to just still yourself
and observe,
to take in both the sky
and the snow—
both argent,
mirrors of one another.

VILLAINY

I was taught as a child
that purple grackles
were squawking villains—
not as upstanding
as the songbirds
with all of their
melodious chirps.

I was taught as a child
that purple grackles
were fit only for scorn
and for accurate shots,
their bleeding feathers
rainbow-hued in the sun.

How wrong we were.
I, for one, hope to be forgiven.

MIDWINTER

A silent house at midwinter—
long curtains closed to the night.

Soft amber light from a lamp—
a glow by which to properly write.

To open a sunrise in my heart—
into the darkness, spilling light.

WITH WHAT WAS THOUGHT TO BE BENEVOLENCE

There was slime coating a struggling trout
in my hands when they were younger.

I released the fish back into the creek,
the cool glittering channel
that had borne it to my spinner's barbs.
My hands were gleaming with water,
and with a protective mucus sheen—
a scent I somehow enjoyed.

I'd thought my deed was benevolent,
smiling boyishly at my own kindness,
until I'd read a short story or poem
a couple of long decades later.

Maybe it was a Hemingway story
or a poem by Raymond Carver.
Either writer would likely be thrilled
at shattering the innocent memory
of a young man, a boy really,
fishing alone in a Wyoming creek.

I hope the trout survived the disease
that my ivory uncalloused hands
bestowed onto its slippery body.
I hope the trout survived
so that it could be caught again—
and devoured.

Did you think that, of all men,
I'd be the one to write of solace?

AN OBLATION

It is for your colorful soul,
that my own soul screams.
I reach for you endlessly,
through clotted darkness,
through filtered rusty light.

My aching heart swells,
pregnant with your image,
with your contours and secrets.
Of you, I am a devotee—
an acolyte of your dogma.

I'm upon your altar.

THE LENGTHS WE ALL GO

The lengths we all go
to locate ourselves,
to unlock the mysteries
that we have buried—

I went to the other side
of our war-torn world,
as an American soldier,
only to find myself.

But I had to be taken
to the soft cusp of death
in order to behold it—
to reach deep and take it.

INVISIBLE WOUNDS

I'm in bed,
wide awake
sometime before sunrise.
My home is silent—
still slumbering
in the predawn dark.
The moon is full—
yellow-white and shining
through the window
like a polished gold coin.
It's an inquisitive moon
that asks important questions.

And just like that,
I find my vaults of memory
have returned me
to the loud cargo bay
of a C-130
that was loaded
with wounded soldiers
and insane soldiers
that had unraveled—
become broken
in the foreign desert heat.

"Why are you here?"
he asked me.

"Why have you left?"

I uttered my reason
with hot shame
that I had cursed myself
to carry forever.
He didn't judge me.
Instead—
he pulled my forehead
into his own,
and he prayed for me.
One of his legs
was riddled
in fresh bullet wounds,
but he was able to discern
my invisible wounds—
and recognize that they
were just as dire,
just as deadly.
Nowhere have I seen
empathy and compassion
in such evidence.
I loved him.

I'm back in my familiar bed,
not the steel-framed bed
of a military psych ward.
She slumbers next to me,
her skin as bare as it was
on our wedding night.
The moon is still gleaming—
lunar fire.
The sky in the window,

beyond the quivering digits
of the empty trees,
is a brightening blue.
If I could pray to anything,
it would be to the sky
and the trees.

Dawn is coming,
and I will rise again.

A GRIEVANCE

I resent the frigid winter
and its ponderous tide
of snow and crunchy ice.

The colorful delicacy
of its quick predecessor—
too brief a seasonal stroke,
was stripped bare,
and ravaged by icy cruelty.

Autumn, I remember you,
and I take care
to be most aware
of your return.

POETIC ENVY
Dedicated to all the Poets

He reads good poetry from a book
until his eyes burn with weariness,
until he wants nothing more than
to cross his arms upon his desk
and sleep a dreamless slumber.

And when he would finally awaken,
his own prose would maybe be better—
half as good as what he'd just read.

IN HINDSIGHT

We would drive down to Denver
almost every single weekend
to visit her hospitalized mother
who'd hurt her brain in a fall.
Her accident had happened
weeks after a terrible storm
that had left our trees broken.
I saw a prologue there—
in hindsight.

She and I would pack the car
and take off into the prairie,
down a straight stretch of highway,
playing Band of Horses albums
because they were a soundtrack
suitable for everything we saw—
for fences of rusty barbed wire
and broad watercolor skies,
for the colossal Rocky Mountains
and the city's urban heart.

What an awful circumstance
for those trips to Colorado,
but somehow, all these years later,
we remember them with fondness.
When I try to think of why that is,
I think it's simply because
we made those trips purely for love.

THINGS TO APPRECIATE

Antique light from an old desk lamp
passing through a glass of bourbon.

A book of poetry in my dry hands,
pages as crisp as the end of summer,
and getting nutrition from poetic lines.

Pipe smoke on a bright autumn day,
mingling with the heady aroma of leaves—
sweater weather; sometimes scarves.

The kind contrast between sunshine,
colored warmly of yellowed cream,
and the blue shadows of a clear day—
crunchy snow smooth upon the ground
in the looming finality of December.

Writing poems in my leather journal,
a cocktail or two prying out words—
extracting ore from worthless stone.

Working at my vintage typewriter,
pounding upon its smooth keys
in the way of my literary idols—

Creating.

    Creating.

        Creating.

94 *Nicholas Trandahl*

SUBTLE STROKES

Creeping through
the cottonwoods
are subtle strokes
of winter morning—

the quietest tide
of buttery light.

Better by which
to see icy flakes
tumbling down
from an empty sky.

CHRONOLOGIC DEATH RATTLE

A slab of fresh months
is birthed anew
in the frosty death
of a tired year.

Timidly whimpering,
these new days
rise from the rime.

THE RUSSIANS

When reading Russian literature,
does the gleam in the broad sky
need to be a particular way?
Does Tolstoy call for lurid grey—
for heavy leaden clouds?
For tension and gloom?

Or does he call for effulgence—
for a warm blaze by which we can
better account for the grand allure
of fair Anna Karénina?

SUMMER IN POKROVSKOE
Dedicated to Leo Tolstoy

Sunbeams slanting
upon the yellow dress
of young Várenka
as she ambles happily
within a meadow
looking for mushrooms—
birches and aspens
towering behind,
and bluish mountains
beyond those trees.

Sergéi watches her
from the wood,
smoking a cigar
to steel himself.

THE GIVER OF GIFTS

It is an evening in January.
I sauté white onions in butter,
but I think of the apple slices
that I scattered in the yard
for roving deer to devour.

We are all equally hungry,
but I've the unnatural ability
to be the giver of gifts.

A POEM FOR CARVER
Dedicated to Raymond Carver

I was parked alongside
a highway in the dusk.
Some whitetail does
were eating grass
right next to my car,
unaware that I
was within.
I was just another piece
of civilization's debris.
One of the does
acted like a buck,
chasing the others away
with her head down,
as if she had antlers.
Maybe, inside,
she felt like a buck.
In making her a doe,
maybe she felt that Nature
had wronged her.

Maybe that's why
she was angry.

STOICISM AND ASSURANCE

There were two golden eagles
sitting on weathered fence posts—
their brown feathers bronzed,
beaten by cold prairie wind.

Stoicism and assurance—
          personified.

QUIETLY NOW

Quietly now.

Please awaken with me,
and greet the new dawn.
It's wreathed in a hush.

A rose blush embellishes
the crystalline purity
of the frosted morning,
stains the murky fog,
pierces, with pinkish hue,
the achromatic setting.

Leafless cottonwoods
are cast in romantic light,
along with the sagebrush
that pepper the frigid plains,
and the rime-dusted back
of a single stealthy deer.

The whole wintry earth
seems fragile enough
to shatter with a shout,
but those jagged shards
wouldn't be any sharper
than the air's bitter bite.

The silhouetted train,
oddly muffled of clamor,
tunnels through the fog.
I am reminded of Tolstoy,
though its cars are laden
with heaps of black coal
in lieu of aristocracy.

This ice-bound morning,
burnished in swelling light,
competes with divinity
for our pious attentions—
undivided.

Quietly now.

ONE'S FIRST CLIMBING TREE

My daughters told me
how our late crabapple tree,
now long sliced down,
was once covered in ladybugs.
They flew from the trunk
to our yellow rose bush.
My daughters were sure
the tree's thick leaves
were made of mint.
I'm sure they thought
that tree was magic—
some fey entity
dwelling in its heart.

There is nothing quite like
the poignant absence
of one's first climbing tree.

THOSE WILD ONES

February feels like November.
These formations
bookend four months
of hushed winter.
And, just like autumn,
the forlorn echoes
of distant geese
trickle in descent
from the grey air—

a rustic music
composed of melodies
that jauntily dance
like fallen leaves—

melodies that
only the wildest
can clearly hear.
They sing of
the southern warmth
and barbaric things—
free things.

I must be becoming
one of those wild ones.
Because when I hear
the returning geese,
I hear the rusty voices
of my oldest friends.

REPLENISHMENT

The light replenishes him
in golden yellow shards,
filtered through old glass,
through dusty lamp shades,
through a tumbler of ice—
        shallow with gin.

The light replenishes him
from cracks dimly glowing,
spreading out underneath—
        ready to give way.

THE BOX MADE OF BONE

At a camp in Qatar
I met a merchant,
a beautiful Muslim woman—
those striking Persian eyes.
She was selling
handmade boxes
constructed of camel bone—
a kaleidoscope
of colored patterns.
I bought one of the boxes
at an exorbitant price
for the American woman
who would soon after
become my ex-wife.
I don't think the box
lacked a single hue.
It wanted for nothing
but a precious thing
to put within it.
After shipping it stateside,
I never saw the box again.
Several things
were about to change.

WHAT I WANT

I want to be in the dim attic
of a weathered old house
somewhere in New England.

Rain is pouring from the clouds
in pure drops, heavy and healthy,
and drumming a cacophony
on a rooftop that is still sound.
It could be summer or early fall.

There are woods all around,
bountiful farmland and orchards.
There are some wild apples
that have fallen in the wet grass.
They shine like colored stones.

This is Transcendentalist country,
a place where Thoreau walked
with a gnarled walking stick
as he looked for perfect apples,
ones suitable for strong cider.

Flashlight in hand, I'm searching,
coughing lightly in the dark attic
from the drifting motes of dust,
through old cardboard boxes
full of linens and vintage items.

That's what I want as I sit here
at my writing desk in Wyoming.

I'm unsure if I'm content or forlorn
as I watch a cold drizzle descend
on this bleached February morn.

JUST AS WELL

Light breaking through Sunday windows—
outside, the light is warm, the air crisp.

My whiskers smell of my pipe smoke,
of black cherries and dark chocolate.
At the church across the quiet street
a pious flock spills out to their cars,
tradition and ceremony still ringing.
I'm watching them, free from judgment.

My friend, his second cigarette burning,
tries to plan a summer camping trip
with me and my wife; all of us are smoking,
our acrid blue-grey banners ascending
into the crystallized morning radiance.

I would rather be camping right now,
wearing woolen layers beside a fire
with nothing but slow-burning promise
written into the day's bucolic agenda.
Instead, on this Sunday, I'm in town
sitting contentedly outside of my home,
scraping blackened dottle out of my pipe
with a pocketknife I got for Christmas.

And I suppose that's just as well.

ARCHITECTURE

The brightening window,
blue with February's ice,
kisses my languid eyes,
eases them open.

She slumbers there,
warm beside me,
so pleasantly familiar
in the dim glow.

My hand locates
the unrivaled curve
of her shapely hip.
I pull us together.

RAIN AND LIGHT

The man and woman,
both in scarves and pea coats,
walk the city streets at night.
Their arms are entwined
and they carry shopping bags—
laden with new dresses for her
and a few new books for him.

A cold rain is heavily pouring
upon the downtown district.
Bronze statues gleam wetly
in the glimmering light
of the amber streetlights
and the long lines of cars
that hiss down the rainy streets.

The rain falls in glinting sheets
like shards of delicate glass
detached from the dark ceiling
of the overcast, late winter sky.
And, like fractured panes of glass,
the rain shatters upon the surfaces
of the sidewalks and the city streets—
the urban rivers of shimmering light.

UNTIL THIS MORNING

Inspired by Gustave Caillebotte's Cliffs by the Sea at Trouville

There are cliffs—
somewhere.
Not here.
Not where I am.
Caillebotte built them
using vibrant oils
exactly a century
before I, wailing,
came into the world
and took my first
tremulous breath.
I had never seen
those coastal cliffs
near Trouville
until this morning—
Wednesday.

Couldn't I be there,
beholden to that vista,
in lieu of
tightening my tie
and stepping into
leather dress shoes
before a day at work?

ANDROMEDA

I read somewhere
that billions of years from now
the Andromeda Galaxy,
that faint amber blur
in the glittering night,
will tear into
our humble Milky Way
and consume it—
a vast cosmic cannibal.

Where will we be then?
Will humanity have long since
wandered curiously out
into the endless gulf of space?
Or will its doom have come early—
before that hungry galaxy
or our own traitorous star
are able to end it all?

I used to daydream of traveling there—
to the Andromeda Galaxy.
Was that an odd thing
for an imaginative child
to dream about?
What an ironic treat then,
that Andromeda will instead
be traveling to me—
across the frigid void.

When that all happens,
that cataclysmic collision,
maybe a part of my spirit
will be here still—
in one form
or another

to see
it all

end.

THINGS REMINDING ME OF OTHER THINGS

The sun was slipping
behind the horizon—
sullen and brown land
smeared with snow.
Crawling lavender clouds
were there as well
to help obfuscate
the evidence of the day.

The night before,
I'd fallen asleep
while I was reading
a new book of poetry.
But that was all right,
because they were good words.

I'm not sure why
that setting sun
reminded me of sleep
and those wonderful poems,
or why I then thought of prayer
when I don't believe in prayers
and haven't prayed
since I was a child—
since the passionless recitation
of toneless verses
within the innumerable masses

of my Catholic days of youth.
I would stand just behind the priest
when I was an altar boy,
swimming in pride and piousness.

But I accept all of these thoughts,
thoughts of sunsets, poems, and prayer.
I accept these thoughts—
and I cherish them.

THUNDER BASIN

A colony of rainstorms
traverse the open prairie,
spilling their handiwork
and sending me a scent
that I've been awaiting
during the fleeting winter.
This feels like the final winter.
Never can I remember rain
on the high Thunder Basin
at the end of February.
Nonetheless, I'm thrilled—
my car windows down,
smelling that rainy, mild air,
upbeat glittering music
bleeding into the twilight.
Later, I'll feel guilty
for tonight's jubilation
in this cancerous world.
But, for now,
let me feel alive.

BELGIUM

The swell of time
is illuminated with
terrible moments—
more being born
each golden morning.
Brussels is screaming,
joining the chorus
of Turkey and Paris,
of New York City and Iraq.
Pain, screams, and tears—
broken glass and stone,
scorched debris,
mangled flesh.

But remember—
love is no illusion,
not some poetic wraith
historically written of
by the romanticists,
a forgotten relic
of a bygone gilded age.
Love is more solid
than anything else—
more eternal.
It will never
be broken into dust
by a wielder of terror.
Somewhere out there,

a rose-colored light
still burns.
We can still find it
in this fog of hate.
It isn't too late.
We can find our way home.

THE ONLY VOICE I HEAR

The smell of rain
has come and gone—
a brief cold wash,
an early spring tempest.
And now—
silence.

Clouds are coming in
from the southeast,
bringing with them
a bitter wind.

It stirs the lone pine
across the street—
its rustling
the only voice I hear.
But that's all right—
isn't it?
The voice of a tree
has never told me
anything mean or hateful.
Their words
are always perfect—
even in misunderstanding.

But these clouds will sour;
these rains
will turn to snow,

and that solitary pine
will get herself
some white lingerie—
a see-through garment,
something that barely covers
her dark body.
Her voice will change then—
her whisper becoming
winter's last hiss.

HORSE THIEF LAKE

A still morning
in the Black Hills.
The ascendant sun
glaring with sudden light
through the mesh door
of the tent.
Slipping outside
to get a fire going
with last night's dim embers.
Writing a short story
in a notebook
while everyone else
slumbers.

Early afternoon—
smoke from the campfire
sliding up the trunk
of a young oak,
its crown
a mane of green leaves.
Through those leaves
is the solstice sun—
shimmering brightly.
Lemon shandy
in a bottle.
Dappled sunlight—
swaying,
the graceful dance

that heralds summer.
Children, like druids,
are harvesting mushrooms
from the emerald vault
of the wood.
They'll roast them
over the fire—
char marks
on the stalks and caps.
Lessons about shelter-building,
about making a campfire.

Reading James Salter
at the lake's edge.
The water is dark.
There are granite cliffs
at the far end of the lake
that people, braver than I,
are hurling themselves from
with glad shrieks
that echo
across the lake.

Driving home—
soiled and weary,
stained with wood smoke.
The way is serpentine,
taking us southwest
through open spaces
painted in verdant green—
charred columns of pine trees

long ago eaten
by a wildfire.
The children are convinced
that old calamity
was the work of a dragon.
I remember a woman
started the fire
about twenty years ago.

At home—
we unpack only ourselves.

PREHISTORIC

What if words
could be trapped
in amber—
all the best ones,
perfect prose,
locked away
in solidity,
in transparency
of golden brown?

And what if
the amber
could be sundered,
spilling out
artful words—

ancient words?

ACKNOWLEDGMENTS

This collection of poems is a harvest sown by many hands, the first of which is my wife Brittany. I'm quite sure I'm a writer because of her support and encouragement. These poems began to bloom immediately after our wedding, and they haven't yet stopped blooming. I'm the most fortunate of writers to be bound in love to my muse.

I also want to thank my parents and the rest of my family and friends. A special acknowledgement goes out to my lovely and talented daughters, who are always so proud and shocked when they discover that other people outside of our household are aware of my writings.

To Pam and Bill Swyers, I want to express my eternal gratitude for giving me my first opportunity to become an author. They reached out and pulled me onto this literary path, and I'm humbled by the faith and support they've always had in my creativity and words.

I want to thank Jessica Kristie for seeing promise in my poetry and allowing me to join the flock at Winter Goose Publishing. To the rest of the goslings at Winter Goose, it's been so fabulous to get to know and be published alongside such a genuinely talented group of authors. Also, a special thank you to my editor, James Koukis, for helping me iron out the wrinkles.

Lastly, I want to show my respect and appreciation to the writers that have shaped me not only as a poet, but also as a man. These writers are Ernest Hemingway, Jim Harrison, and Raymond Carver (the three of which taught me that simplicity and honesty were more powerful than metaphor); James Salter (who taught me the sensuality of language); Mary Oliver and Henry David Thoreau (both of which grew verdant woods upon my soul); and Leo Tolstoy (who found it within himself to write the single finest piece of literature known to man).

ABOUT THE AUTHOR

Nicholas Trandahl is an avid outdoorsman and credits his many adventures and travels as the prime source of inspiration for his writings. One is just as likely to find him on a trail or beside a trout stream as sitting at his writing desk with his old typewriter, a family heirloom. Trandahl writes at the edge of the Black Hills of Wyoming, where he lives with his wife and children.

CPSIA information can be obtained
at www.ICGtesting.com
Printed in the USA
FSHW02n2205190918
52144FS